easy

Chicken

# easy

## Chicken

Love Food ® is an imprint of Parragon Books Ltd

Parragon
Queen Street House
4 Queen Street
Bath BA1 1HE, UK

Copyright © Parragon Books Ltd 2007

Designed by Mark Cavanagh
Additional Photography by Günter Beer
Additional Food Styling by Oliver Trific
Introduction by Anne Sheasby

Love Food ® and the accompanying heart device is a trademark of Parragon Books Ltd.

ISBN: 978-1-4075-2355-2

Printed in China

NOTES FOR THE READER
• This book uses imperial, metric, and US cup measurements. Follow the same units of measurement
throughout; do not mix imperial and metric.
• All spoon measurements are level: teaspoons are assumed to be 5 ml, and tablespoons are assumed
to be 15 ml.
• Unless otherwise stated, milk is assumed to be lowfat and eggs are medium. The times given are an
approximate guide only.
• Some recipes contain nuts. If you are allergic to nuts you should avoid using them and any products
containing nuts.
• Recipes using raw or very lightly cooked eggs should be avoided by infants, the elderly, pregnant
women, convalescents, and anyone suffering from illness.

# Contents

# Introduction

Chicken is one of the most popular meats as it is versatile, easy to prepare, quick to cook, and full of flavor. This makes it ideal as the basis for numerous tasty recipes to suit all occasions.

Chicken is an excellent source of protein and provides some vitamins such as Niacin (a B vitamin), and minerals such as zinc and iron (in the dark meat). It is also low in fat, especially when the skin is removed.

## Buying Chicken

Most supermarkets and butchers offer a good range of chicken. When buying fresh chicken, it is advisable to look for free-range birds because their flavor is often superior to that of intensively reared chicken. They will also have enjoyed a good standard of welfare, with some access to open air. Organic birds are preferred by some consumers, although they are usually the most expensive choice.

Check the "use by" date and choose a bird with plump breasts (rather than one that looks bony), with a firm, unblemished creamy white or yellow skin (depending on the variety). Larger birds tend to be meatier with a more developed flavor.

Buying a whole bird and cutting it into portions yourself is usually the cheapest option. However, for convenience, you may prefer to buy chicken portions (either with skin or skinned, with bones or boneless), such as chicken breast portions, drumsticks, thighs, and wings.

## Storage & Food Safety

Store fresh chicken in a loosely covered container in the refrigerator for up to 2 days. Make sure that any raw chicken is placed on a low shelf (to prevent it from dripping or leaking onto any foods below) in the coldest part of your refrigerator, which should be between 32°F and 41°F (0°C and 5°C). Remember that raw and cooked chicken should always be stored separately.

Fresh raw chicken can be frozen for up to 3 months and cooked chicken can be frozen for up to 2 months.

Ideally, frozen chicken should be thawed in the refrigerator, not at room temperature, to minimize possible bacterial contamination. Thaw frozen chicken overnight in the refrigerator and always make sure it is thoroughly thawed before you cook it (otherwise the center may not be cooked when the outside looks done, which may lead to food poisoning). Remember, never refreeze thawed chicken.

Always wash your hands thoroughly before and after handling raw or cooked chicken, and make sure that kitchen counters and utensils are cleaned with hot soapy water. Always use separate cutting boards and utensils when preparing raw and cooked chicken.

## Roasting Chicken

Prepare, then weigh the whole bird (with the stuffing in place if the bird is going to be roasted stuffed), and calculate the cooking time, allowing 20 minutes per 1 lb/450 g, plus 20 minutes. Roast in a preheated oven at 425°F/220°C, for the first 15 minutes, then reduce the oven temperature to 375°F/190°C for the remaining calculated time. Roast for the calculated time or until the juices run clear when the thickest part of the thigh is pierced with a fork or skewer. If the juices are pink or there are traces of blood, continue roasting the chicken until the juices run clear. Remove the chicken from the roasting pan and place on a warmed serving plate. Cover with foil and let rest for 10 minutes before carving.

The internal temperature of cooked chicken should reach 176–185°F (80–85°C).

Chicken portions can be roasted at 375°F/190°C for 30–45 minutes, depending on their size. Always make sure the chicken is thoroughly cooked before serving.

## Adding Flavor to Roast Chicken

When roasting a whole chicken, there are several simple ways you can add flavor to the meat. For example, place a whole lemon (pierced a couple of times), a peeled onion, or a few fresh herbs and peeled garlic cloves inside the cavity of the bird before roasting. Alternatively, carefully push citrus fruit slices (such as lemon, orange, or lime slices) or fresh herb sprigs (such as thyme or rosemary) under the skin covering the breast, before roasting.

Flavored butters can also be spread under the skin. Alternatively, try brushing the outside of a whole chicken with oil, then sprinkling with ground spices or dried herbs to add flavor, color, and crispness.

# Soups &
# Appetizers

# Cream of Chicken Soup

*serves 4*

3 tbsp butter

4 shallots, chopped

1 leek, sliced

1 lb/450 g skinless,boneless chicken breasts, chopped

2½ cups chicken stock

1 tbsp chopped fresh parsley

1 tbsp chopped fresh thyme, plus extra sprigs to garnish

¾ cup heavy cream

salt and pepper

Melt the butter in a large pan over medium heat. Add the shallots and cook, stirring, for 3 minutes, until slightly softened. Add the leek and cook for another 5 minutes, stirring. Add the chicken, stock, and herbs, and season to taste with salt and pepper. Bring to a boil, then lower the heat and simmer for 25 minutes, until the chicken is tender and cooked through. Remove from the heat and let cool for 10 minutes.

Transfer the soup into a food processor or blender and process until smooth (you may need to do this in batches). Return the soup to the rinsed-out pan and warm over low heat for 5 minutes.

Stir in the cream and cook for another 2 minutes, then remove from the heat and ladle into warmed serving bowls. Garnish with sprigs of thyme and serve immediately.

# Chicken Noodle Soup

serves 4

2 skinless, boneless
chicken breasts

5 cups water or chicken
stock

3 carrots, peeled and cut
into $^1/_4$-inch/5-mm slices

3 oz/85 g vermicelli
(or other fine noodles)

salt and pepper

fresh tarragon leaves,
to garnish

Place the chicken breasts in a large saucepan, add the water, and bring to a simmer. Cook for 25–30 minutes. Skim any foam from the surface, if necessary. Remove the chicken from the stock and keep warm.

Continue to simmer the stock, add the carrots and vermicelli, and cook for 4–5 minutes.

Thinly slice or shred the chicken breasts and place in warmed serving dishes.

Season the soup to taste with salt and pepper and pour over the chicken. Serve immediately, garnished with the tarragon.

# Thai Chicken Soup

*serves 4*

1 tbsp sesame oil or chili oil

2 garlic cloves, chopped

2 scallions, trimmed and sliced

1 leek, trimmed and finely sliced

1 tbsp grated fresh ginger

1 red chile, seeded and finely chopped

12 oz/350 g skinless, boneless chicken breasts, cut into strips

scant 3½ cups chicken stock

2 tbsp rice wine

1 tbsp chopped lemongrass

6 kaffir lime leaves, finely shredded

7 oz/200 g fine egg noodles

salt and pepper

Heat the oil in a wok or large pan. Add the garlic and cook over medium heat, stirring, for 1 minute, then add the scallions, leek, ginger, and chile and cook, stirring, for another 3 minutes. Add the chicken, stock, and rice wine, bring to a boil, and simmer for 20 minutes. Stir in the lemon grass and lime leaves.

Bring a separate pan of water to a boil and add the noodles. Cook for 3 minutes, drain well, then add them to the soup. Season to taste with salt and pepper. Cook for another 2 minutes. Remove from the heat, ladle into warmed serving bowls, and serve hot.

# Chicken & Broccoli Soup

*serves 4–6*

8 oz/225 g head of broccoli

4 tbsp unsalted butter

1 onion, chopped

generous ⅛ cup basmati rice

8 oz/225 g skinless, boneless chicken breast, cut into thin slivers

scant ¼ cup all-purpose whole wheat flour

1¼ cups milk

2 cups chicken stock

generous ⅓ cup corn kernels

salt and pepper

Break the broccoli into small florets and cook in a pan of lightly salted boiling water for 3 minutes, drain, then plunge into cold water and set aside.

Melt the butter in a pan over medium heat, add the onion, rice, and chicken, and cook for 5 minutes, stirring frequently.

Remove the pan from the heat and stir in the flour. Return to the heat and cook for 2 minutes, stirring constantly. Stir in the milk and then the stock. Bring to a boil, stirring constantly, then reduce the heat and let simmer for 10 minutes.

Drain the broccoli and add to the pan with the corn and salt and pepper to taste. Let simmer for 5 minutes, or until the rice is tender, then serve.

# Chicken & Rice Soup

*serves 4*

6¾ cups chicken stock

2 small carrots, very thinly sliced

1 celery stalk, finely diced

1 baby leek, halved lengthwise and thinly sliced

4 oz/115 g petit pois, defrosted if frozen

1 cup cooked rice

5½ oz/150 g cooked chicken, sliced

2 tsp chopped fresh tarragon

1 tbsp chopped fresh flat-leaf parsley, plus sprigs to garnish

salt and pepper

Put the stock in a large saucepan and add the carrots, celery, and leek. Bring to a boil, reduce the heat to low, and simmer gently, partially covered, for 10 minutes.

Stir in the petit pois, rice, and chicken and continue cooking for an additional 10–15 minutes, or until the vegetables are tender.

Add the chopped tarragon and parsley, then taste and adjust the seasoning, adding salt and pepper as needed.

Ladle the soup into warmed serving bowls, garnish with sprigs of parsley and serve immediately.

# Chicken & Potato Soup with Bacon

*serves 4*

1 tbsp butter

2 garlic cloves, chopped

1 onion, sliced

9 oz/250 g smoked lean bacon, chopped

2 large leeks, sliced

2 tbsp all-purpose flour

4 cups chicken stock

1 lb 12 oz/800 g potatoes, chopped

7 oz/200 g skinless boneless chicken breast, chopped

4 tbsp heavy cream

salt and pepper

broiled bacon, to garnish

Melt the butter in a large pan over medium heat. Add the garlic and onion and cook, stirring, for 3 minutes, until slightly softened. Add the chopped bacon and leeks and cook for another 3 minutes, stirring.

In a bowl, mix the flour with enough stock to make a smooth paste and stir it into the pan. Cook, stirring, for 2 minutes. Pour in the remaining stock, then add the potatoes and chicken. Season to taste with salt and pepper. Bring to a boil, then lower the heat and simmer for 25 minutes, until the chicken and potatoes are tender and cooked through.

Stir in the cream and cook for another 2 minutes, then remove from the heat and ladle into warmed serving bowls. Garnish with broiled bacon and serve immediately.

# Chicken Liver Pâté

*serves 4–6*

1 cup butter

8 oz/225 g trimmed chicken livers, thawed if frozen

2 tbsp Marsala or brandy

1½ tsp chopped fresh sage

1 garlic clove, coarsely chopped

⅔ cup heavy cream

salt and pepper

fresh bay leaves or sage leaves, for garnish

crackers, for serving

Melt 3 tablespoons of the butter in a large, heavy-bottom skillet. Add the chicken livers and cook over medium heat for about 4 minutes on each side. They should be browned on the outside but still pink in the middle. Transfer to a food processor and process until finely chopped.

Stir the Marsala or brandy into the skillet, scraping up any sediment with a wooden spoon, then add to the food processor with the sage, garlic, and 1/2 cup of the remaining butter. Process until smooth. Add the cream, season to taste with salt and pepper, and process until thoroughly combined and smooth. Spoon the pâté into a dish or individual ramekins, level the surface, and let cool completely.

Melt the remaining butter, then spoon it over the surface of the pâté. Decorate with bay leaves, cool, then let chill in the refrigerator. Serve with crackers.

# Chicken Satay

*serves 4*

4 tbsp smooth peanut butter

heaping ⅓ cup soy sauce

4 skinless, boneless chicken breasts, cut into thin strips

*to serve*

freshly cooked rice of your choice

lemon wedges

Preheat the broiler. Mix the peanut butter and soy sauce together in a bowl until smooth. Stir in the chicken strips, tossing well to coat in the mixture.

Thread the chicken strips onto 4 presoaked, wooden skewers and broil for about 5 minutes on each side until cooked through. Serve immediately with freshly cooked rice and lemon wedges.

# Chicken Balls with Dipping Sauce

*serves 4*

2 large skinless, boneless chicken breasts

3 tbsp vegetable oil

2 shallots, finely chopped

½ celery stalk, finely chopped

1 garlic clove, crushed

2 tbsp light soy sauce

1 small egg

1 bunch of scallions

salt and pepper

*for the dipping sauce*

3 tbsp dark soy sauce

1 tbsp rice wine

1 tsp sesame seeds

Cut the chicken into ¾-inch/2-cm pieces. Heat half of the oil in a skillet or wok and stir-fry the chicken over high heat for 2–3 minutes until golden. Remove from the skillet or wok with a slotted spoon and set aside.

Add the shallots, celery, and garlic to the skillet or wok and stir-fry for 1–2 minutes until softened.

Place the chicken, shallots, celery, and garlic in a food processor and process until finely ground. Add 1 tablespoon of the light soy sauce and just enough egg to make a fairly firm mixture. Season to taste with salt and pepper.

Trim the scallions and cut into 2-inch/5-cm lengths. Make the dipping sauce by mixing together the dark soy sauce, rice wine, and sesame seeds in a small serving bowl and set aside.

Shape the chicken mixture into 16–18 walnut-size balls. Heat the remaining oil in the skillet or wok and stir-fry the chicken balls in small batches for 4–5 minutes until golden brown. As each batch is cooked drain on paper towels and keep hot.

Add the scallions to the skillet or wok and stir-fry for 1–2 minutes until they begin to soften, then stir in the remaining light soy sauce. Serve the chicken balls with the stir-fried scallions and the bowl of dipping sauce.

# Sesame Chicken Wings

*makes 24*

4 tbsp olive oil, plus extra for oiling

finely grated rind and juice of 2 lemons

1 tbsp light brown sugar

pinch of cayenne pepper, or to taste

24 chicken wings, any small hairs removed and the thin tips cut off

2 tbsp sesame seeds

salt and pepper

Preheat the oven to 400°F/200°C and line a roasting pan with foil. Put a broiler rack in the pan.

Put the oil in a bowl, add the lemon rind and juice, sugar, cayenne pepper, and salt and pepper to taste and stir until the sugar has dissolved. Add the chicken wings and use your hands to coat well with the marinade. At this point, you can cook the wings immediately or cover and let marinate in the refrigerator for several hours.

Generously brush the broiler rack with oil. Arrange the wings on the rack in a single layer and sprinkle with the sesame seeds. If your broiler rack isn't large enough to hold all the wings, cook in batches. Roast in the preheated oven for 25–30 minutes, until the juices run clear when a skewer is inserted into the thickest part of the chicken, and the skin is crisp. Transfer to a plate lined with crumpled paper towels and let cool before serving.

# Chicken Crostini

*serves 4*

12 slices French bread or country bread

4 tbsp olive oil

2 garlic cloves, chopped

2 tbsp finely chopped fresh oregano

3½ oz/100 g cold roast chicken, cut into small, thin slices

4 tomatoes, sliced

12 thin slices of goat cheese

12 black olives, pitted and chopped

salt and pepper

fresh red and green salad leaves, to serve

Put the bread under a preheated medium broiler and lightly toast on both sides. Meanwhile, pour the olive oil into a bowl and add the garlic and oregano. Season with salt and pepper and mix well. Remove the toasted bread slices from the broiler and brush them on one side only with the oil mixture.

Place the bread slices, oiled sides up, on a cookie sheet. Put some sliced chicken on top of each one, followed by a slice of tomato.

Divide the slices of goat cheese among the bread slices, then top with the chopped olives. Drizzle over the remaining oil mixture and transfer to a preheated oven, 350°F/180°C. Bake for about 5 minutes, or until the cheese is golden and starting to melt.

Remove from the oven and serve on a bed of fresh red and green salad leaves.

# Curried Chicken with Grapes

*serves 6*

4 tbsp olive oil

2 lb/900 g skinless, boneless chicken meat, diced

²/₃ cup diced, rindless, smoked bacon,

12 shallots

2 garlic cloves, chopped finely

1 tbsp mild curry powder

1¼ cups mayonnaise

1 tbsp honey

1 tbsp chopped fresh flat-leaf parsley

pepper

½ cup pitted white grapes, quartered, to garnish

cold saffron rice, to serve

Heat the oil in a large skillet and add the chicken, bacon, shallots, garlic, and curry powder. Cook slowly, stirring, for about 15 minutes.

Spoon the mixture into a clean mixing bowl. Allow to cool completely, then season to taste with pepper.

Blend the mayonnaise with the honey, then add the parsley. Toss the chicken mixture in the mayonnaise mixture.

Place the chicken in a serving dish, garnish with the grapes, and serve with cold saffron rice.

# Chicken Livers in Red Wine & Thyme

*serves 4*

9 oz/250 g fresh
chicken livers

3 tbsp lemon-flavored oil

2 garlic cloves,
finely chopped

4 tbsp red wine

1 tbsp chopped
fresh thyme

salt and pepper

arugula leaves, to serve

sprigs of fresh thyme,
to garnish

Rinse the chicken livers under cold running water and pat dry with paper towels. Heat the lemon-flavored oil in a skillet. Add the garlic and cook, stirring, over medium heat for 2 minutes. Add the chicken livers, wine, and chopped thyme. Season to taste with salt and pepper and cook for 3 minutes.

Meanwhile, arrange the arugula leaves on a large serving platter. Remove the pan from the heat and spoon the chicken livers over the bed of arugula. Pour over the cooking juices, then garnish with sprigs of fresh thyme and serve immediately.

# Chicken, Cheese & Arugula Salad

*serves 4*

5½ oz/150 g arugula leaves

2 celery stalks, trimmed and sliced

½ cucumber, sliced

2 scallions, trimmed and sliced

2 tbsp chopped fresh parsley

¼ cup walnut pieces

12 oz/350 g boneless roast chicken, sliced

4½ oz/125 g bleu cheese, cubed

handful of seedless red grapes, cut in half (optional)

salt and pepper

*for the dressing*

2 tbsp olive oil

1 tbsp sherry vinegar

1 tsp whole grain mustard

1 tbsp chopped fresh mixed herbs

Wash the arugula leaves, pat dry with paper towels, and put them into a large salad bowl. Add the celery, cucumber, scallions, parsley, and walnuts and mix together well. Transfer to a large serving platter. Arrange the chicken slices over the salad, then scatter over the bleu cheese. Add the grapes, if using. Season well with salt and pepper.

To make the dressing, put all the ingredients into a screw-top jar and shake well. Alternatively, put them into a bowl and mix together well. Drizzle the dressing over the salad and serve.

# Smoked Chicken & Cranberry Salad

*serves 4*

1 smoked chicken, weighing 3 lb/1.3 kg

scant 1 cup dried cranberries

2 tbsp apple juice or water

7 oz/200 g sugar snap peas

2 ripe avocados

juice of ½ lemon

4 lettuce hearts

1 bunch of watercress, trimmed

2 oz/55 g arugula

½ cup walnuts, chopped, to garnish (optional)

*for the dressing*

2 tbsp olive oil

1 tbsp walnut oil

2 tbsp lemon juice

1 tbsp chopped fresh mixed herbs, such as parsley and lemon thyme

salt and pepper

Carve the chicken carefully, slicing the white meat. Divide the legs into thighs and drumsticks and trim the wings. Cover with plastic wrap and refrigerate.

Put the cranberries in a bowl. Stir in the apple juice, then cover with plastic wrap and let soak for 30 minutes.

Meanwhile, blanch the sugar snap peas, then refresh under cold running water and drain.

Peel, pit, and slice the avocados, and toss in the lemon juice to prevent browning.

Separate the lettuce hearts and arrange on a large serving platter with the avocados, sugar snap peas, watercress, arugula, and chicken.

Put all the dressing ingredients, including salt and pepper to taste, in a screw-top jar, then screw on the lid and shake until well blended.

Drain the cranberries and mix them with the dressing, then pour over the salad.

Serve immediately, scattered with walnuts, if using.

# Chicken & Spinach Salad

*serves 4*

3 celery stalks, thinly sliced

½ cucumber, thinly sliced

2 scallions, thinly sliced

9 oz/250 g young spinach leaves

3 tbsp chopped fresh flat-leaf parsley

12 oz/350 g roast chicken, thinly sliced

smoked almonds, to garnish (optional)

*for the dressing*

1-inch/2.5-cm piece of fresh ginger, finely grated

3 tbsp olive oil

1 tbsp white wine vinegar

1 tbsp honey

½ tsp ground cinnamon

salt and pepper

Toss the celery, cucumber, and scallions in a large bowl with the spinach leaves and parsley.

Transfer to serving plates and arrange the chicken on top of the salad.

In a screw-topped jar, combine all the dressing ingredients, including salt and pepper to taste, shake well to mix, and pour it over the salad. Sprinkle with a few smoked almonds, if using.

# Waldorf Chicken Salad

*serves 4*

1 lb 2 oz/500 g red dessert apples, diced

3 tbsp fresh lemon juice

²/₃ cup light mayonnaise

1 head celery

4 shallots, sliced

1 garlic clove, finely chopped

¾ cup walnuts, chopped, plus extra to garnish

1 lb 2 oz/500 g cooked chicken, cubed

1 romaine lettuce

pepper

Place the apples in a bowl with the lemon juice and 1 tablespoon of the mayonnaise. Leave for 40 minutes.

Using a sharp knife, slice the celery very thinly. Add the celery, shallots, garlic, and walnuts to the apples and mix together. Stir in the remaining mayonnaise and blend thoroughly.

Add the chicken, season to taste with pepper and mix with the other ingredients.

Line a serving dish with the lettuce. Pile the chicken salad into the dish, garnish with chopped walnuts and serve.

# Cajun Chicken Salad

*serves 4*

4 skinless, boneless chicken breasts, about 5 oz/ 140 g each

4 tsp Cajun seasoning

2 tsp corn oil

1 ripe mango, peeled, pitted, and cut into thick slices

7 oz/200 g mixed salad greens

1 red onion, halved and thinly sliced

6 oz/175 g cooked beet, diced

3 oz/85 g radishes, sliced

generous ⅜ cup walnut halves

2 tbsp sesame seeds

*for the dressing*

4 tbsp walnut oil

1–2 tsp whole grain mustard

1 tbsp lemon juice

salt and pepper

Make 3 diagonal slashes across each chicken breast. Put the chicken into a shallow dish and sprinkle all over with the Cajun seasoning. Cover and let chill for at least 30 minutes.

When ready to cook, brush a stove-top grill pan with the corn oil. Heat over high heat until very hot and a few drops of water sprinkled into the pan sizzle immediately. Add the chicken and cook for 7–8 minutes on each side, or until thoroughly cooked. If still slightly pink in the center, cook a little longer. Remove the chicken and set aside.

Add the mango slices to the pan and cook for 2 minutes on each side. Remove and set aside.

Meanwhile, arrange the salad greens in a serving bowl and sprinkle over the onion, beet, radishes, and walnut halves.

Put the walnut oil, mustard, lemon juice, and salt and pepper to taste in a screw-top jar and shake until well blended. Pour over the salad and sprinkle with the sesame seeds.

Cut the reserved chicken into thick slices. Arrange the mango and the salad on a serving plate and top with the chicken breast and a few of the salad greens.

2

# Light Bites

# Mediterranean Chicken Baguette

*serves 2*

1 garlic clove, halved

1 large baguette stick, cut lengthwise

½ cup olive oil

2 oz/55 g cold roast chicken, thinly sliced

2 large tomatoes, sliced

¾ oz/20 g canned anchovy fillets, drained

8 large pitted black olives, chopped

pepper

Rub the garlic over the insides of the bread and sprinkle with the oil.

Arrange the chicken on top of the bread. Place the tomatoes and anchovies on top of the chicken.

Scatter with the black olives, and season with plenty of black pepper. Sandwich the loaf back together and wrap tightly in foil until required. Cut into slices to serve.

# Open Chicken Sandwiches

serves 6

3 hard-cooked eggs, the yolk mashed and the white chopped

2 tbsp butter, softened

2 tbsp mustard

1 tsp anchovy extract

2 cups grated Cheddar cheese

3 cooked skinless, boneless chicken breasts, diced

6 thick slices of rustic bread, buttered

12 slices each of tomato and cucumber

pepper

In a large bowl, mix the egg yolks and whites with the butter, mustard, and anchovy extract, and season to taste with pepper.

Mix in the Cheddar and chicken, and spread the mixture on the bread.

Make alternate rows of the egg yolk and the egg white on top of the chicken mixture. Arrange the tomato and cucumber slices on top and serve.

# Smoked Chicken & Ham Focaccia

*serves 2–4*

1 thick focaccia loaf (about 6–7 inches)

handful of basil leaves

2 small zucchini, coarsely shredded

6 wafer-thin slices of smoked chicken

6 wafer-thin slices of cooked ham

8 oz/225 g Taleggio cheese, cut into strips

freshly grated nutmeg (optional)

cherry tomatoes, to serve (optional)

Preheat a grill pan under the broiler until both broiler and grill pan are hot. If you do not have a grill pan, heat a heavy baking sheet or roasting pan instead. Slice the thick focaccia in half horizontally and cut the top half into strips.

Cover the bottom half of the focaccia with basil leaves, top with the zucchini in an even layer, and then cover with the chicken and ham, alternating the slices, and wrinkling them. Lay the strips of focaccia on top, placing strips of Taleggio cheese between them. Sprinkle with a little nutmeg, if using.

Place the assembled bread on the hot grill pan and cook under the broiler, well away from the heat, for about 5 minutes, until the Taleggio has melted, and the top of the bread is browned. Serve immediately with cherry tomatoes, if liked.

# Chicken Wraps

*serves 4*

²/₃ cup plain yogurt

1 tbsp whole grain mustard

10 oz/280 g cooked
skinless, boneless
chicken breast, diced

5 oz/140 g iceberg lettuce,
finely shredded

3 oz/85 g cucumber,
thinly sliced

2 celery stalks, sliced

½ cup black seedless
grapes, halved

8 x 8-inch/20-cm soft flour
tortillas or 4 x 10-inch/
25-cm soft flour tortillas

pepper

Combine the yogurt and mustard in a bowl and season to taste with pepper. Stir in the chicken and toss until thoroughly coated.

Put the lettuce, cucumber, celery, and grapes into a separate bowl and mix well.

Fold a tortilla in half and in half again to make a cone that is easy to hold. Half-fill the tortilla pocket with the salad mixture and top with some of the chicken mixture. Repeat with the remaining tortillas, salad, and chicken. Serve at once.

# Cheese & Chicken Toasts

*serves 4*

2 cups grated crumbly cheese

1⅓ cups cooked chicken, shredded

1 tbsp butter

1 tbsp Worcestershire sauce

1 tsp dry mustard

2 tsp all-purpose flour

4 tbsp mild beer

4 slices of bread

salt and pepper

cherry tomatoes, to serve

Place the crumbly cheese, chicken, butter, Worcestershire sauce, mustard, all-purpose flour, and beer in a small pan. Mix all the ingredients together, then season to taste with salt and pepper.

Gently bring the mixture to a boil and remove from the heat immediately.

Using a wooden spoon, beat until the mixture becomes creamy in texture. Let it cool.

Once the chicken mixture has cooled, toast the bread on both sides and spread with the chicken mixture.

Place under a hot broiler and broil until bubbling and golden brown.

Serve with cherry tomatoes.

# Spicy Chicken Muffins

*makes 12*

½ cup sunflower-seed or peanut oil, plus extra for oiling

2 onions, chopped

3 scallions, chopped

1 small fresh red chile, seeded and finely chopped

3 skinless, boneless chicken thighs, chopped into small pieces

1 tsp paprika

scant 2¼ cups self-rising flour

1 tsp baking powder

2 large eggs

1 tbsp lemon juice

1 tbsp grated lemon rind

½ cup sour cream

½ cup plain yogurt

salt and pepper

Preheat the oven to 375°F/190°C. Oil a 12-cup muffin pan with sunflower-seed oil. Heat a little of the remaining oil in a skillet, add the onions, scallions, and chile, and cook over low heat, stirring constantly, for 3 minutes. Remove from the heat, lift out the onions, scallions, and chile, and set aside. Heat a little more of the remaining oil in the skillet, add the chicken and paprika, and cook, stirring, over medium heat for 5 minutes. Remove from the heat and set aside.

Sift the flour and baking powder into a large mixing bowl. In a separate bowl, lightly beat the eggs, then stir in the remaining oil and the lemon juice and rind. Pour in the sour cream and the yogurt and mix together. Add the egg mixture to the flour mixture, then gently stir in the onions, scallions, chile, and chicken. Season to taste with salt and pepper. Do not overstir the batter – it is fine for it to be a little lumpy.

Divide the muffin batter evenly among the 12 cups in the muffin pan (they should reach the top), then transfer to the oven. Bake for 20 minutes, or until risen and golden. Remove the muffins from the oven and serve warm, or place them on a cooling rack and let cool.

# Chicken Fajitas

*serves 4*

3 tbsp olive oil, plus extra for drizzling

3 tbsp maple syrup or honey

1 tbsp red wine vinegar

2 garlic cloves, crushed

2 tsp dried oregano

1–2 tsp dried red pepper flakes

4 skinless, boneless chicken breasts

2 red bell peppers, seeded and cut into 1-inch/ 2.5-cm strips

salt and pepper

warmed flour tortillas and shredded lettuce, to serve

Place the oil, maple syrup, vinegar, garlic, oregano, pepper flakes, and salt and pepper to taste in a large, shallow dish or bowl and mix together.

Slice the chicken across the grain into slices 1 inch/2.5 cm thick. Toss in the marinade until well coated. Cover and let chill in the refrigerator for 2–3 hours, turning occasionally.

Heat a grill pan until hot. Lift the chicken slices from the marinade with a slotted spoon, lay on the grill pan, and cook over a medium–high heat for 3–4 minutes on each side, or until cooked through. Remove the chicken to a warmed plate and keep warm.

Add the bell peppers, skin-side down, to the grill pan and cook for 2 minutes on each side. Transfer to the plate.

Divide the chicken and peppers among the flour tortillas, top with a little shredded lettuce, wrap and serve immediately.

# Chicken & Chile Enchiladas

*serves 4*

corn oil, for brushing

5 fresh hot green chiles, such as jalapeño, seeded and chopped

1 Spanish onion, chopped

2 garlic cloves, chopped

2 tbsp chopped fresh cilantro

2 tbsp lime juice

½ cup chicken stock

2 beefsteak tomatoes, peeled, seeded, and chopped

pinch of sugar

12 oz/350 g cooked chicken, shredded

¾ cup queso anejo or Cheddar cheese, grated

2 tsp chopped fresh oregano

8 corn or flour tortillas

salt

Preheat the oven to 350°F/180°C and brush a large, ovenproof dish with oil. Place two-thirds of the chiles, the onion, garlic, cilantro, lime juice, stock, tomatoes, and sugar in a food processor and pulse to a purée. Scrape into a pan and let simmer over medium heat for 10 minutes, until thickened.

Mix the remaining chiles, the chicken, ½ cup of the cheese and the oregano together. Season with salt and stir in half the sauce.

Heat the tortillas in a dry, heavy-bottom skillet or in the microwave according to the package instructions. Divide the chicken mixture among them, spooning it along the centers, then roll up and place, seam-side down, in the dish.

Pour the remaining sauce over the enchiladas and sprinkle with the remaining cheese. Bake in the preheated oven for 20 minutes and serve hot.

# The Ultimate Chicken Burger

*serves 4*

4 large skinless, boneless
chicken breasts

1 large egg white

1 tbsp cornstarch

1 tbsp all-purpose flour

1 egg, beaten

1 cup fresh white
breadcrumbs

2 tbsp corn oil

2 beefsteak tomatoes,
sliced

*to serve*

4 burger buns, sliced

shredded lettuce

mayonnaise

Place the chicken breasts between 2 sheets of nonstick parchment paper and flatten slightly using a meat mallet or a rolling pin. Beat the egg white and cornstarch together, then brush over the chicken. Cover and let chill for 30 minutes, then coat in the flour.

Place the egg and breadcrumbs in 2 separate bowls and coat the burgers first in the egg, allowing any excess to drip back into the bowl, then in the breadcrumbs.

Heat a heavy-bottom skillet and add the oil. When hot, add the burgers and cook over medium heat for 6–8 minutes on each side, or until thoroughly cooked. If you are in doubt, it is worth cutting one of the burgers in half. If there is any sign of pinkness, cook for a little longer. Add the tomato slices for the last 1–2 minutes of the cooking time to heat through.

Serve the burgers in the burger buns with the tomato slices, a little shredded lettuce and a spoonful of mayonnaise.

# Bacon-Wrapped Chicken Burgers

*serves 4*

1 lb/450 g fresh ground chicken

1 onion, grated

2 garlic cloves, crushed

3/8 cup pine nuts, toasted

1/2 cup Gruyère cheese, grated

2 tbsp fresh snipped chives

salt and pepper

2 tbsp whole wheat flour

8 lean Canadian bacon slices

1–2 tbsp corn oil

*to serve*

salad leaves

slices of red onion

4 ciabatta rolls

Place the ground chicken, onion, garlic, pine nuts, cheese, chives, and salt and pepper in a food processor. Using the pulse button, blend the mixture together using short sharp bursts. Scrape out onto a board and shape into 4 even-size burgers. Coat in the flour, then cover and let chill for 1 hour.

Wrap each burger with 2 bacon slices, securing in place with a wooden toothpick.

Heat a heavy-bottom skillet and add the oil. When hot, add the burgers and cook over medium heat for 5–6 minutes on each side, or until thoroughly cooked through. Serve the burgers in ciabatta rolls, dressed with salad leaves and onion slices.

# Chicken & Herb Fritters

*makes 8*

1 lb 2 oz/500 g mashed potato, with butter added

1⅓ cups cooked chicken, chopped

⅔ cups cooked ham, finely chopped

1 tbsp fresh mixed herbs

2 eggs, lightly beaten

1 tbsp milk

2 cups fresh brown breadcrumbs

oil, for shallow-frying

salt and pepper

mixed salad, to serve

In a large bowl, blend the potatoes, chicken, ham, herbs, and 1 egg, and season to taste with salt and pepper. Shape the mixture into small balls or flat pancakes.

Add the milk to the second egg.

Place the breadcrumbs on a plate. Dip the balls in the egg and milk mixture and roll in the breadcrumbs, to coat them completely.

Heat the oil in a large skillet and cook the fritters until golden brown. Serve hot with a mixed salad.

# Baked Potatoes with Chicken

*serves 4*

4 large baking potatoes

9 oz/250 g cooked chicken, cubed

4 scallions, thickly sliced

1 cup soft cheese

pepper

mixed salad, to serve

Preheat the oven to 400°F/200°C. Bake the potatoes in the preheated oven for about 60 minutes, until tender, or cook in a microwave on high power for 12–15 minutes.

Mix the chicken and scallions with the soft cheese.

Cut a cross into the top of each potato and squeeze slightly apart. Spoon the chicken filling into the potatoes and season to taste with black pepper to taste. Serve immediately with a mixed salad.

# Chicken Kabobs in a Yogurt Marinade

*serves 4*

1¼ cups Greek-style yogurt

2 garlic cloves, crushed

juice of ½ lemon

1 tbsp chopped fresh herbs such as oregano, dill, tarragon, or parsley

4 large skinless, boneless chicken breasts

salt and pepper

*to serve*

cooked rice

shredded lettuce

lemon wedges

To make the sauce, put the yogurt, garlic, lemon juice, herbs, and salt and pepper to taste in a large bowl and mix well together.

Cut the chicken breasts into chunks measuring about 1½ inches/4 cm square. Add to the yogurt mixture and toss well together until the chicken pieces are coated. Cover and leave to marinate in the fridge for about 1 hour. If you are using wooden skewers, soak them in cold water for 30 minutes.

Preheat the broiler. Thread the pieces of chicken onto 8 flat, greased, metal kabob skewers, wooden skewers, or rosemary stems and place on a greased broiler pan.

Cook the kabobs under the preheated broiler for about 15 minutes, turning and basting occasionally with the remaining marinade, until lightly browned and tender. Serve the kabobs on a bed of rice and shredded lettuce with lemon wedges for squeezing over.

# Spicy Tomato Chicken Kabobs

*serves 4*

1 lb 2 oz/500 g skinless, boneless chicken breast portions

3 tbsp tomato paste

2 tbsp honey

2 tbsp Worcestershire sauce

1 tbsp chopped fresh rosemary

9 oz/250 g cherry tomatoes

sprigs of fresh rosemary, to garnish

couscous or rice, to serve

If you are using wooden skewers, soak them in cold water for 30 minutes. Cut the chicken into 1-inch/2.5-cm chunks and place in a bowl.

Combine the tomato paste, honey, Worcestershire sauce, and chopped rosemary in a small bowl. Add to the chicken, stirring to coat evenly.

Preheat the broiler. Alternating the chicken pieces and cherry tomatoes, thread them onto 8 metal kabob skewers or pre-soaked wooden skewers.

Spoon over any remaining glaze. Cook under the preheated broiler for about 8–10 minutes, turning occasionally, until the chicken is thoroughly cooked.

Serve with couscous or rice and garnish with sprigs of rosemary.

# Skewered Chicken Spirals

*serves 4*

4 skinless, boneless chicken breast portions

1 garlic clove, crushed

2 tbsp tomato paste

4 slices smoked lean bacon

large handful of fresh basil leaves

vegetable oil, for brushing

salt and pepper

salad, to serve

If you are using wooden skewers, soak them in cold water for 30 minutes. Spread out a piece of chicken between two sheets of plastic wrap and beat firmly with a rolling pin or meat mallet to flatten the chicken to an even thickness. Repeat with the remaining chicken.

Combine the garlic and tomato paste and spread the mixture over the chicken. Lay a bacon slice over each, then sprinkle with the basil. Season to taste with salt and pepper.

Roll up each piece of chicken firmly, then cut into thick slices. Thread the slices onto 4 metal kabob skewers or presoaked wooden skewers to hold the chicken in a spiral shape.

Brush lightly with oil and cook under a preheated broiler for about 10 minutes, turning once. Serve hot with salad.

# Fettuccine with Chicken & Basil Pesto

*serves 4*

2 tbsp vegetable oil

4 skinless, boneless chicken breasts

12 oz/350 g dried fettuccine

salt and pepper

sprig of fresh basil, to garnish

*for the pesto*

1²⁄₃ cups shredded fresh basil

½ cup extra virgin olive oil

3 tbsp pine nuts

3 garlic cloves, crushed

½ cup freshly grated Parmesan cheese

2 tbsp freshly grated Romano cheese

salt

To make the pesto, put the basil, olive oil, pine nuts, garlic, and a generous pinch of salt in a food processor or blender. Process the ingredients until smooth. Scrape the mixture into a bowl and stir in the cheeses.

Heat the vegetable oil in a skillet over medium heat. Cook the chicken breasts, turning once, for 8–10 minutes, or until the juices are no longer pink. Cut into small cubes.

Meanwhile, bring a large saucepan of lightly salted water to a boil. Add the pasta, bring back to a boil, and cook for 8–10 minutes, or until tender but still firm to the bite. Drain and transfer to a warmed serving dish. Add the chicken and pesto, then season to taste with pepper. Toss well to mix.

Garnish with a sprig of basil and serve warm.

# Five-Spice Chicken with Vegetables

*serves 4*

2 tbsp sesame oil

1 garlic clove, chopped

3 scallions, trimmed and sliced

1 tbsp cornstarch

2 tbsp rice wine

4 skinless, boneless chicken breasts, cut into strips

1 tbsp Chinese five-spice powder

1 tbsp grated fresh ginger

1/2 cup chicken stock

3 1/2 oz/100 g baby corn cobs, sliced

3 cups bean sprouts

finely chopped scallions, to garnish (optional)

freshly cooked jasmine rice, to serve

Heat the oil in a preheated wok or large skillet. Add the garlic and scallions and stir-fry over medium–high heat for 1 minute.

In a bowl, mix together the cornstarch and rice wine, then add the mixture to the pan. Stir-fry for 1 minute, then add the chicken, five-spice powder, ginger, and chicken stock and cook for another 4 minutes. Add the corn cobs and cook for 2 minutes, then add the bean sprouts and cook for another minute.

Remove from the heat, garnish with chopped scallions, if using, and serve with freshly cooked jasmine rice.

# Chicken & Peanut Stir-Fry

*serves 4*

2 tbsp peanut oil

1 garlic clove, chopped

3 scallions, trimmed and sliced

4 skinless, boneless chicken breasts, cut into bite-size chunks

1 tbsp grated fresh ginger

½ tsp chili powder

5½ oz/150 g sugar snap peas, trimmed

4½ oz/125 g baby corn cobs

2 tbsp smooth peanut butter

1 tbsp light soy sauce

freshly cooked rice, to serve

Heat the oil in a preheated wok or large skillet. Add the garlic and scallions and stir-fry over medium–high heat for 1 minute. Add the chicken, ginger, and chili powder and stir-fry for 4 minutes. Add the sugar snap peas and baby corn cobs and cook for 2 minutes.

In a bowl, mix together the peanut butter and soy sauce, then add it to the wok. Stir-fry for another minute.

Remove from the heat, pile onto 4 serving dishes, and serve with freshly cooked rice.

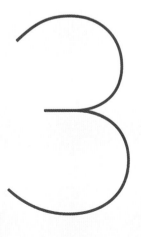

# Main
# Courses

# Potato, Leek & Chicken Pie

*serves 4*

8 oz/225 g waxy potatoes, cubed

5 tbsp butter

1 skinless, boneless chicken breast, about 6 oz/175 g, cubed

1 leek, sliced

2 cups sliced crimini mushrooms

2½ tbsp all-purpose flour

1¼ cups milk

1 tbsp whole grain mustard

2 tbsp chopped fresh sage

8 oz/225 g filo dough, thawed if frozen

3 tbsp melted butter

salt and pepper

Cook the potato cubes in a pan of boiling water for 5 minutes. Drain and set aside.

Melt the butter in a skillet and cook the chicken cubes for 5 minutes or until browned all over.

Add the leek and mushrooms and cook for 3 minutes, stirring. Stir in the flour and cook for 1 minute stirring constantly. Gradually stir in the milk and bring to a boil. Add the mustard, sage, and potato cubes and simmer for 10 minutes.

Meanwhile, line a deep pie dish with half of the sheets of filo dough. Spoon the sauce into the dish and cover with 1 sheet of dough. Brush the dough with butter and lay another sheet on top. Brush this sheet with butter.

Cut the remaining filo dough into strips and fold them onto the top of the pie to create a ruffled effect. Brush the strips with the melted butter and cook in a preheated oven, 350°F/180°C, for 45 minutes or until golden brown and crisp. Serve hot.

# Chicken Nuggets with Dipping Sauce

*serves 4*

3 skinless, boneless
chicken breasts

4 tbsp whole wheat flour

1 tbsp wheat germ

½ tsp ground cumin

½ tsp ground coriander

1 egg, lightly beaten

2 tbsp olive oil

pepper

*for the dipping sauce*

3½ oz/100 g sunblush
tomatoes

3½ oz/100 g fresh
tomatoes, peeled,
seeded, and chopped

2 tbsp mayonnaise

Preheat the oven to 375°F/190°C. Cut the chicken breasts into 1½-inch/4-cm chunks. Mix the flour, wheat germ, cumin, coriander, and pepper to taste, in a bowl, then divide in half and put on 2 separate plates. Put the beaten egg on a third plate.

Pour the oil into a baking sheet with a rim and heat in the oven. Roll the chicken pieces in one plate of flour, shake to remove any excess, then roll in the egg and in the second plate of flour, again shaking off any excess flour. When all the nuggets are ready, remove the baking sheet from the oven and toss the nuggets in the hot oil. Roast in the oven for 25–30 minutes until golden and crisp.

Meanwhile, to make the dipping sauce, put both kinds of tomatoes in a blender or food processor and process until smooth. Add the mayonnaise and process again until well combined.

Remove the nuggets from the oven and drain on paper towels. Serve with the dipping sauce.

# Cheddar-Baked Chicken

*serves 4*

1 tbsp milk

2 tbsp mustard

1 cup grated Cheddar

3 tbsp all-purpose flour

2 tbsp chopped fresh chives

4 skinless, boneless chicken breasts

salad leaves, to serve

Preheat the oven to 400°F/200°C. Mix together the milk and mustard in a bowl. In another bowl, combine the cheese, flour, and chives.

Dip the chicken breasts into the milk and mustard mixture, brushing to coat evenly.

Dip the chicken breasts into the cheese mixture, pressing to coat evenly. Place on a cookie sheet and spoon any spare cheese coating over the top.

Bake in the preheated oven for 30–35 minutes, until golden brown and the juices run clear, not pink, when a skewer is inserted into the thickest part of the meat. Serve the chicken hot with salad leaves.

# Crispy-Coated Chicken Breasts with Wedges

*serves 4*

*for the sweet potato wedges*

4 large sweet potatoes, peeled and cut into wedges

4 tbsp vegetable oil

1 tsp chili powder

*for the crispy-coated chicken*

1¾ oz/50 g hazelnuts, toasted and ground

3 tbsp dried white or whole wheat breadcrumbs

2 tbsp freshly grated Romano cheese

1 tbsp chopped fresh parsley

4 skinless chicken breasts

1 egg, beaten

4 tbsp vegetable oil

salt and pepper

sprigs of fresh parsley, to garnish

lemon wedges, to serve

Preheat the oven to 400°F/200°C. To make the sweet potato wedges, bring a large pan of water to a boil. Add the potatoes and cook over medium heat for 5 minutes. Drain well. Pour 2 tablespoons of the oil into a large bowl and stir in the chili powder. Add the potatoes and turn in the mixture until coated. Transfer to a cookie sheet, drizzle over the remaining oil, and bake for 35–40 minutes, turning frequently, until golden and cooked through.

About 15 minutes before the end of the cooking time, put the hazelnuts, breadcrumbs, cheese, and parsley into a bowl, season, and mix. Dip the chicken breasts into the egg, then coat in the breadcrumb mixture.

Heat the oil in a skillet. Add the chicken and cook over medium heat for 3–4 minutes on each side until golden. Lift out and drain on paper towels.

Remove the potatoes from the oven, divide among 4 serving plates, and add a chicken breast to each. Garnish with parsley and serve with lemon wedges.

# Chicken Tikka Masala

*serves 4–6*

2 tbsp ghee or vegetable or peanut oil

1 large garlic clove, finely chopped

1 red chile, seeded and chopped

2 tsp ground cumin

2 tsp ground paprika

½ tsp salt

14 oz/400 g canned chopped tomatoes

1¼ cups heavy cream

8 pieces cooked tandoori chicken

pepper

sprigs of fresh cilantro, to garnish

To make the tikka masala, heat the ghee in a large skillet with a lid over medium heat. Add the garlic and chile and stir-fry for 1 minute. Stir in the cumin, paprika, salt, and pepper to taste and continue stirring for about 30 seconds.

Stir the tomatoes with their juice and the cream into the pan. Reduce the heat to low and let the sauce simmer for about 10 minutes, stirring frequently, until it reduces and thickens.

Meanwhile, remove all the bones and any skin from the tandoori chicken pieces, then cut the meat into bite-size pieces.

Adjust the seasoning of the sauce, if necessary. Add the chicken pieces to the pan, cover, and let simmer for 3–5 minutes, until the chicken is heated through. Sprinkle with the sprigs of cilantro and serve with freshly cooked rice.

# Chicken Pepperonata

*serves 4*

8 skinless chicken thighs

2 tbsp whole wheat flour

2 tbsp olive oil

1 small onion, sliced thinly

1 garlic clove, crushed

1 each large red, yellow, and green bell peppers, seeded and thinly sliced

14 oz/400 g canned chopped tomatoes

1 tbsp chopped fresh oregano, plus extra to garnish

salt and pepper

crusty whole wheat bread, to serve

Toss the chicken thighs in the flour, shaking off the excess.

Heat the oil in a wide skillet and cook the chicken quickly until sealed and lightly browned, then remove from the pan.

Add the onion to the pan and cook gently until soft. Add the garlic, bell peppers, tomatoes, and oregano, then bring to a boil, stirring.

Arrange the chicken over the vegetables, season well with salt and pepper, then cover the pan tightly and simmer for 20–25 minutes or until the chicken is completely cooked and tender.

Taste and adjust the seasoning, if necessary, garnish with oregano, and serve with crusty whole wheat bread.

# Mexican Drumsticks

*serves 4*

2 tbsp oil

8 chicken drumsticks

1 onion, finely chopped

1 tsp chili powder

1 tsp ground coriander

14 oz/400 g canned chopped tomatoes

2 tbsp tomato paste

²/₃ cup frozen corn

salt and pepper

mixed bell pepper salad, to serve

Heat the oil in a large skillet. Add the chicken drumsticks and cook over a medium heat until lightly browned. Remove the chicken drumsticks from the pan with a draining spoon and set aside until required.

Add the onion to the pan and cook for 3–4 minutes, until softened, then stir in the chili powder and ground coriander and cook for a few seconds, stirring briskly so the spices do not burn. Add the tomatoes and the tomato paste and stir well to combine.

Return the chicken drumsticks to the pan and simmer gently for 20 minutes, until the chicken is tender and thoroughly cooked. Add the corn and cook for another 3–4 minutes. Season to taste with salt and pepper.

Serve hot with a mixed bell pepper salad.

# Roasted Chicken &
# Sweet Potatoes

*serves 4*

8 chicken thighs

1 red onion, minced

8 tbsp tomato ketchup

2 tbsp maple syrup

1 tbsp Worcestershire sauce

1 tbsp whole grain mustard

1 garlic clove, minced

3 tbsp olive oil

4 sweet potatoes, peeled and cut into chunks

Preheat the oven to 400°F/200°C. Score each chicken thigh 2–3 times.

Mix together all the remaining ingredients, except the sweet potatoes, in a large bowl. Add the chicken and toss well to coat. Cover with plastic wrap and let marinate in a cool place for 20 minutes, then add the sweet potatoes and toss well to coat.

Tip the chicken and sweet potatoes into a baking dish and roast in the preheated oven for 40–50 minutes until well browned. The chicken should be tender and the juices run clear when a skewer is inserted into the thickest part of the meat.

Serve immediately.

# Thai Chicken

*serves 4*

6 garlic cloves, coarsely chopped

1 tsp black pepper

8 chicken legs

1 tbsp Thai fish sauce

4 tbsp dark soy sauce

fresh ginger cut into matchsticks, to garnish

Put the garlic cloves in a mortar, add the pepper and pound to a paste with a pestle. Using a sharp knife, make 3 to 4 diagonal slashes on both sides of the chicken legs. Spread the garlic paste over the chicken legs and place them in a dish. Add the fish sauce and soy sauce and turn the legs to coat well. Cover with plastic wrap and let marinate in the refrigerator for 2 hours.

Preheat the broiler. Drain the chicken legs, setting aside the marinade. Put them on a broiler rack and cook under the broiler, turning and basting frequently with the reserved marinade, for 20 to 25 minutes, or until cooked through and tender. The juices should run clear when a skewer is inserted into the thickest part of the meat. Serve immediately garnished with the ginger.

# Broiled Chicken with Lemon

*serves 4*

4 chicken quarters

grated rind and juice of
2 lemons

4 tbsp olive oil

2 garlic cloves, crushed

2 sprigs of fresh thyme,
plus extra to garnish

salt and pepper

Prick the skin of the chicken quarters all over with a fork. Put the chicken pieces in a dish, add the lemon juice, oil, garlic, thyme, and salt and pepper to taste and mix well. Cover and let marinate in the fridge for at least 2 hours.

To cook the chicken, preheat the broiler. Put the chicken in a broiler pan and baste with the marinade. Cook for 30–40 minutes, basting and turning occasionally, until the chicken is tender. Serve hot garnished with the grated lemon rind and sprigs of thyme.

# Jerk Chicken

*serves 4*

2 red chiles

2 tbsp corn oil, plus extra
for brushing

2 garlic cloves, finely
chopped

1 tbsp finely chopped onion

1 tbsp finely chopped
scallion

1 tbsp white wine vinegar

1 tbsp lime juice

2 tsp raw brown sugar

1 tsp dried thyme

1 tsp ground cinnamon

1 tsp ground allspice

¼ tsp freshly grated
nutmeg

4 chicken quarters

salt and pepper

*to garnish*
sprigs of fresh cilantro
lime wedges

Seed and finely chop the red chiles, then place them in a small glass bowl with the oil, garlic, onion, scallion, vinegar, lime juice, raw brown sugar, thyme, cinnamon, allspice, and nutmeg. Season to taste with salt and pepper and mash thoroughly with a fork.

Using a sharp knife, make a series of diagonal slashes in the chicken pieces and place them in a large, shallow, nonmetallic dish. Spoon the jerk seasoning over the chicken, rubbing it well into the slashes. Cover and let marinate in the refrigerator for up to 8 hours.

Preheat the broiler. Remove the chicken from the marinade, discarding the marinade, brush with oil and cook under the preheated broiler, turning frequently, for 30–35 minutes. Transfer to plates and serve garnished with sprigs of cilantro and lime wedges.

# Mustard & Honey Drumsticks

serves 4

8 chicken drumsticks

sprigs of fresh parsley,
to garnish

for the glaze

4 tbsp honey

4 tbsp whole grain mustard

4 tbsp white wine vinegar

2 tbsp corn oil

salt and pepper

Using a sharp knife, make 2–3 diagonal slashes in the chicken drumsticks and place them in a large, nonmetallic dish.

Mix all the ingredients for the glaze together in a measuring cup, seasoning to taste with salt and pepper. Pour the glaze over the drumsticks, turning until the drumsticks are well coated. Cover with plastic wrap and let marinate in the refrigerator for at least 1 hour.

Preheat the broiler. Drain the chicken drumsticks, reserving the marinade. Cook the chicken under the preheated broiler, turning frequently and brushing with the reserved marinade, for 25–30 minutes, or until thoroughly cooked. Transfer to serving plates, garnish with sprigs of parsley, and serve immediately.

# Sticky Lime Chicken

*serves 4*

4 part-boned, skinless chicken breasts, about 5 oz/140 g each

grated rind and juice of 1 lime

1 tbsp honey

1 tbsp olive oil

1 garlic clove, chopped (optional)

1 tbsp chopped fresh thyme, plus extra sprigs to garnish

pepper

roasted cherry tomatoes, to serve

Preheat the oven to 375°F/190°C. Arrange the chicken breasts in a shallow roasting pan.

Put the lime rind and juice, honey, oil, garlic, if using, and thyme in a small bowl and combine thoroughly. Spoon the mixture evenly over the chicken breasts and season to taste with pepper.

Roast the chicken in the preheated oven, basting every 10 minutes, for 35–40 minutes, or until the chicken is tender and the juices run clear when a skewer is inserted into the thickest part of the meat. As the chicken cooks, the liquid in the pan will thicken to give a sticky coating.

Garnish with sprigs of thyme and serve with roasted cherry tomatoes.

# Sweet & Sour Chicken

*serves 4*

4 skinless, boneless chicken breasts

½ cup all-purpose flour

2 tbsp olive oil

2 large garlic cloves, chopped

1 bay leaf

1 tbsp grated fresh ginger

1 tbsp chopped fresh lemongrass

4 tbsp sherry vinegar

5 tbsp rice wine or sherry

1 tbsp honey

1 tsp chili powder

½ cup orange juice

4 tbsp lime juice

salt and pepper

wedges of lime, to garnish

freshly cooked noodles, to serve

Season the chicken breasts on both sides with salt and pepper to taste, then roll them in the flour until coated. Heat the oil in a large skillet. Add the garlic and cook, stirring, over medium heat for 1 minute. Add the chicken, bay leaf, ginger, and lemongrass and cook for 2 minutes on each side.

Add the vinegar, rice wine, and honey, bring to a boil, then lower the heat and simmer, stirring occasionally, for 10 minutes. Add the chili powder, then stir in the orange juice and lime juice. Simmer for another 10 minutes. Using a perforated spoon, lift out the chicken and set aside. Strain and reserve the liquid and discard the bay leaf, then return the liquid to the pan with the chicken. Simmer for another 15–20 minutes.

Remove from the heat and transfer to individual serving plates. Serve with freshly cooked noodles and garnish with lime wedges.

# Chicken Chow Mein

*serves 4*

9 oz/250 g medium egg
noodles

2 tbsp sunflower oil

9 oz/250 g cooked chicken
breasts, shredded

1 garlic clove, finely
chopped

1 red bell pepper, seeded
and thinly sliced

3½ oz/100 g shiitake
mushrooms, sliced

6 scallions, sliced

1 cup beansprouts

3 tbsp soy sauce

1 tbsp sesame oil

Place the egg noodles in a large bowl or dish and break
them up slightly. Pour enough boiling water over the
noodles to cover and leave to stand while preparing the
other ingredients.

Heat the sunflower oil in a large preheated wok. Add the
chicken, garlic, bell pepper, mushrooms, scallions, and
beansprouts to the wok and stir-fry for about 5 minutes.

Drain the noodles thoroughly. Add the noodles to the wok,
toss well, and stir-fry for a further 5 minutes.

Drizzle the soy sauce and sesame oil over the chow mein
and toss until well combined. Transfer to warmed serving
bowls and serve immediately.

# Cajun Chicken Gumbo

*serves 2*

1 tbsp sunflower oil

4 chicken thighs

1 small onion, diced

2 celery stalks, diced

1 small green bell pepper, seeded and diced

½ cup long-grain rice

1¼ cups chicken stock

1 small red chile, sliced thinly

9 oz/250 g okra

1 tbsp tomato paste

salt and pepper

Heat the oil in a wide pan and sauté the chicken until golden. Remove the chicken from the pan using a draining spoon. Stir in the onion, celery, and green bell pepper and sauté for 1 minute. Pour off any excess fat.

Add the rice and sauté, stirring briskly, for another 1 minute. Add the chicken stock and bring to the boil.

Add the chile and okra to the pan with the tomato paste. Season to taste with salt and pepper.

Return the chicken to the pan and stir. Cover tightly and simmer gently for 15 minutes, or until the rice is tender, the chicken is done, and all the liquid has been absorbed. Stir occasionally and if the gumbo becomes too dry, add a little extra stock to moisten. Serve immediately.

# Chicken & Spinach Lasagne

*serves 4*

12 oz/350 g frozen chopped spinach, thawed and drained

½ tsp ground nutmeg

1 lb/450 g lean cooked chicken, diced

4 sheets no-precook lasagna verde

1½ tbsp cornstarch

scant 2 cups milk

4 tbsp freshly grated Parmesan cheese

salt and pepper

*for the tomato sauce*

14 oz/400 g canned chopped tomatoes

1 medium onion, finely chopped

1 garlic clove, crushed

⅔ cup white wine

3 tbsp tomato paste

1 tsp dried oregano

salt and pepper

Preheat the oven to 400°F/200°C.

To make the tomato sauce, place the tomatoes in a pan and stir in the onion, garlic, wine, tomato paste, and oregano. Bring to a boil and simmer for 20 minutes until thick. Season to taste with salt and pepper.

Drain the spinach again and pat dry on paper towels. Arrange the spinach in the base of an ovenproof dish. Sprinkle with nutmeg and season to taste.

Arrange the diced chicken over the spinach and spoon the tomato sauce over it. Arrange the sheets of lasagna over the tomato sauce.

Blend the cornstarch with a little of the milk to make a paste. Pour the remaining milk into a pan and stir in the cornstarch paste. Heat gently for 2–3 minutes, stirring constantly, until the sauce thickens. Season to taste with salt and pepper.

Spoon the sauce over the lasagna to cover it completely and transfer the dish to a cookie sheet. Sprinkle the grated cheese over the sauce and bake in the preheated oven for 25 minutes until golden brown and bubbling. Serve immediately.

# Mediterranean Chicken Parcels

*serves 6*

1 tbsp olive oil

6 skinless, boneless chicken breasts

2 cups mozzarella cheese, sliced

3½ cups sliced zucchini

6 large tomatoes, sliced

pepper

1 small bunch of fresh basil leaves, torn

Preheat the oven to 400°F/200°C.

Cut 6 pieces of foil each about 10-inches/25-cm square. Brush the foil squares lightly with oil and set aside until required.

With a sharp knife, slash each chicken breast at intervals and place the mozzarella between the cuts in the chicken.

Divide the zucchini and tomatoes between the pieces of foil, and season with pepper to taste. Scatter the basil over the vegetables in each package.

Place the chicken on top of each pile of vegetables, then wrap in the foil to enclose the chicken and vegetables, tucking in the ends.

Place on a cookie sheet and bake in the preheated oven for about 30 minutes.

Unwrap each foil package and serve.

4

# Entertaining

# Roast Chicken

*serves 6*

1 chicken, weighing
5 lb/2.25 kg

4 tbsp butter

2 tbsp chopped fresh
thyme

1 lemon, quartered

½ cup white wine

salt and pepper

6 sprigs of fresh thyme,
to garnish

Preheat the oven to 425°F/220°C. Make sure the chicken is clean, wiping it inside and out using paper towels, and place in a roasting pan.

Place the butter in a bowl and soften with a fork, then mix in the chopped thyme and season well with salt and pepper. Butter the chicken all over with the herb butter, inside and out, and place the lemon quarters inside the body cavity. Pour the wine over the chicken.

Roast the chicken in the center of the oven for 15 minutes. Reduce the temperature to 375°F/190°C and continue to roast for an additional 1¾ hours, basting frequently. Cover with foil if the skin starts to brown too much. If the pan dries out, add a little more wine or water.

Test that the chicken is cooked by piercing the thickest part of the leg with a sharp knife or skewer and making sure the juices run clear. Remove from the oven.

Remove the chicken from the roasting pan and place on a warmed serving plate to rest, covered with foil, for 10 minutes before carving.

Place the roasting pan on top of the stove and heat the pan juices gently over low heat, until they have reduced and are thick and glossy.

Serve the chicken with the pan juices and sprinkle with the thyme sprigs.

# Coq au Vin

*serves 4*

¼ cup butter

2 tbsp olive oil

4 lb/1.8 kg chicken pieces

4 oz/115 g rindless smoked bacon, cut into strips

4 oz/115 g pearl onions, peeled

4 oz/115 g cremini mushrooms, halved

2 garlic cloves, finely chopped

2 tbsp brandy

scant 1 cup red wine

1¼ cups chicken stock

1 bouquet garni

2 tbsp all-purpose flour

salt and pepper

bay leaves, to garnish

Melt half the butter with the oil in a large, flameproof casserole. Add the chicken and cook over medium heat, stirring, for 8–10 minutes, or until golden brown. Add the bacon, onions, mushrooms, and garlic.

Pour in the brandy and set it alight with a match or taper. When the flames have died down, add the wine, stock, and bouquet garni and season to taste with salt and pepper. Bring to a boil, reduce the heat, and simmer gently for 1 hour, or until the chicken pieces are cooked through and tender. Meanwhile, make a beurre manié by mashing the remaining butter with the flour in a small bowl.

Remove and discard the bouquet garni. Transfer the chicken to a large plate and keep warm. Stir the beurre manié into the casserole, a little at a time. Bring to a boil, return the chicken to the casserole, and serve immediately, garnished with bay leaves.

# Chicken Cacciatore

*serves 4*

1 roasting chicken, about
3 lb 5 oz, cut into 6 or 8
serving pieces

1 cup all-purpose flour

3 tbsp olive oil

⅔ cup dry white wine

1 green bell pepper, seeded
and sliced

1 red bell pepper, seeded
and sliced

1 carrot, finely chopped

1 celery stalk, finely
chopped

1 garlic clove, crushed

7 oz/200 g canned chopped
tomatoes

salt and pepper

Rinse and pat dry the chicken pieces with paper towels.
Lightly dust them with seasoned flour.

Heat the oil in a large skillet. Add the chicken and fry over a
medium heat until browned all over; remove from the pan
and set aside.

Drain off all but 2 tablespoons of the fat in the pan. Add the
wine and stir for a few minutes. Then add the bell peppers,
carrot, celery, and garlic and season with salt and pepper to
taste. Simmer together for about 15 minutes.

Add the tomatoes to the pan. Cover and simmer for
30 minutes, stirring often, until the chicken is completely
cooked through.

Check the seasoning before serving piping hot.

# Chicken with Forty Cloves of Garlic

*serves 6*

1 chicken, weighing 3 lb 8 oz/1.6 kg

3 garlic bulbs, separated into cloves but unpeeled

6 fresh thyme sprigs

2 fresh tarragon sprigs

2 bay leaves

1¼ cups dry white wine

salt and pepper

green beans, to serve

Preheat the oven to 350°F/180°C. Season the chicken inside and out with salt and pepper, then truss with fine string or elastic string. Place on a rack in a casserole dish and arrange the garlic and herbs round it.

Pour the wine over the chicken and cover with a tight-fitting lid. Cook in the oven for 1½–1¾ hours, or until tender and the juices run clear when a skewer or the tip of a sharp knife is inserted into the thickest part of the meat.

Transfer the chicken and garlic to a dish and keep warm. Strain the cooking juices into a pitcher. Carve the meat. Skim off any fat on the surface of the cooking juices.

Divide the chicken and garlic between serving plates. Spoon over a little of the cooking juices. Serve immediately with green beans, handing round the remaining cooking juices separately.

# Chicken Kiev

*serves 6*

4 oz/115 g butter, softened

3–4 garlic cloves, very finely chopped

1 tbsp chopped fresh parsley

1 tbsp chopped fresh chives

finely grated rind and juice of ½ lemon

8 skinless boneless chicken breasts, about 4 oz/115 g each

⅜ cup all-purpose flour

2 eggs, lightly beaten

1½ cups uncolored dry breadcrumbs

peanut or corn oil, for deep-frying

salt and pepper

Beat the butter in a bowl with the garlic, herbs, lemon rind, and juice. Season to taste with salt and pepper. Divide into 8 pieces, then shape into cylinders. Wrap in foil and let chill until firm (about 2 hours).

Place the chicken between 2 sheets of plastic wrap. Pound gently with a rolling pin until evenly thin. Place a butter cylinder on each chicken piece and roll up. Secure with toothpicks.

Place the flour, eggs, and breadcrumbs in separate shallow dishes. Dip the rolls into the flour, then into the eggs and, finally, the breadcrumbs. Place on a plate, cover, and let chill for 1 hour.

Heat the oil in a pan or deep-fryer to 350°F/180°C, or until a cube of bread browns in 30 seconds. Deep-fry the chicken in batches for 8–10 minutes, or until cooked through and golden brown. Drain on paper towels. Serve immediately.

Divide the chicken and garlic between serving plates. Spoon over a little of the cooking juices. Serve immediately with green beans, handing round the remaining cooking juices separately.

# Green Chicken Curry

*serves 4*

2 tbsp peanut or vegetable oil

4 scallions, coarsely chopped

2 tbsp green curry paste

3 cups canned coconut milk

1 chicken bouillon cube

6 skinless, boneless chicken breasts, about 4 oz/115 g each, cut into 1-inch/2.5-cm cubes

large handful of fresh cilantro, chopped

1 tsp salt

cooked rice or noodles, to serve

Heat the oil in a preheated wok. Add the scallions and stir-fry over medium–high heat for 30 seconds, or until starting to soften.

Add the curry paste, coconut milk, and bouillon cube and bring gently to a boil, stirring occasionally. Add the chicken cubes, half the cilantro, and the salt and stir well. Reduce the heat and simmer gently for 8–10 minutes, or until the chicken is cooked through and tender. Stir in the remaining cilantro. Serve immediately with rice or noodles.

# Chicken Tagine

*serves 4*

1 tbsp olive oil

1 onion, cut into small wedges

2–4 garlic cloves, sliced

1 lb/450 g skinless, boneless chicken breast, diced

1 tsp ground cumin

2 cinnamon sticks, lightly bruised

1 tbsp whole wheat flour

8 oz/225 g eggplant, diced

1 red bell pepper, seeded and chopped

3 oz/85 g button mushrooms, sliced

1 tbsp tomato paste

2½ cups chicken stock

10 oz/280 g canned chickpeas, drained and rinsed

⅓ cup no-soak dried apricots, chopped

salt and pepper

1 tbsp chopped fresh cilantro

Heat the oil in a large pan over medium heat, add the onion and garlic and cook for 3 minutes, stirring frequently. Add the chicken and cook, stirring constantly, for an additional 5 minutes, or until sealed on all sides. Add the cumin and cinnamon sticks to the pan halfway through sealing the chicken.

Sprinkle in the flour and cook, stirring constantly, for 2 minutes.

Add the eggplant, red bell pepper, and mushrooms and cook for an additional 2 minutes, stirring constantly.

Blend the tomato paste with the stock, stir into the pan, and bring to a boil. Reduce the heat and add the chickpeas and apricots. Cover and let simmer for 15–20 minutes, or until the chicken is tender.

Season with salt and pepper to taste and serve immediately, sprinkled with cilantro.

# Chicken Risotto

*serves 4*

4 tbsp butter

1 onion, chopped

4½ oz/125 g skinless chicken breasts, chopped

12 oz/350 g risotto rice

1 tsp turmeric

1¼ cups white wine

5 cups hot chicken stock

2¾ oz/75 g crimini mushrooms, sliced

1¾ oz/50 g cashews, broken in half

salt and pepper

arugula, to serve

shavings of fresh Parmesan cheese and fresh basil leaves, to garnish

Melt the butter in a large pan over medium heat. Add the onion and cook, stirring, for 1 minute. Add the chicken and cook, stirring, for another 5 minutes.

Add the rice and cook, stirring, for 15 minutes. Then add the turmeric, season with salt and pepper, and mix well. Gradually stir in the wine, then stir in the hot stock, a ladleful at a time, waiting for each ladleful to be absorbed before stirring in the next. Simmer for 20 minutes, stirring from time to time, until the rice is tender and nearly all of the liquid has been absorbed. If necessary, add a little more stock to prevent the risotto from drying out. Stir in the mushrooms and cashews, and cook for another 3 minutes.

Arrange the arugula on 4 individual serving plates. Remove the risotto from the heat and spoon it over the arugula. Scatter over the Parmesan shavings and basil leaves and serve at once.

# Chicken with Linguine & Artichokes

*serves 4*

4 chicken breasts, skinned

finely grated rind and juice of 1 lemon

2 tbsp olive oil

2 garlic cloves, crushed

14 oz/400 g canned artichoke hearts, drained and sliced

9 oz/250 g baby plum tomatoes

10½ oz/300 g dried linguine

chopped fresh flat-leaf parsley and Parmesan cheese, finely grated, to serve

Put each chicken breast between 2 pieces of plastic wrap and pound lightly to flatten. Put the chicken into a shallow, nonmetallic dish with the lemon rind and juice and 1 tablespoon of the oil and turn to coat in the marinade. Cover and let marinate in the refrigerator for 30 minutes.

Put a large pan of water on to boil. Heat the remaining oil in a skillet over low heat, add the garlic, and cook for 1 minute, stirring frequently. Add the artichokes and tomatoes and cook for 5 minutes, stirring occasionally. Add about half the marinade from the chicken and cook over medium heat for an additional 5 minutes. Cook the linguine in the boiling water for 7–9 minutes, or until just tender.

Meanwhile, preheat the broiler to high. Remove the chicken from the remaining marinade and arrange on the broiler pan. Cook the chicken under the preheated broiler for 5 minutes each side, until thoroughly cooked.

Drain the pasta and return to the pan, pour over the artichoke and tomato mixture, and slice in the cooked chicken.

Divide among 4 warmed serving plates and sprinkle over the parsley and cheese.

# Buttered Chicken Parcels

*serves 4*

4 tbsp butter

4 shallots, finely chopped

10½ oz/300 g frozen spinach, thawed

1 lb/450 g bleu cheese, crumbled

1 egg, lightly beaten

1 tbsp chopped fresh chives

1 tbsp chopped fresh oregano

pepper

4 large, skinless chicken breasts

8 slices prosciutto

fresh chives, to garnish

baby spinach leaves, to serve

Melt half of the butter in a skillet over medium heat. Add the shallots and cook, stirring, for 4 minutes. Remove from the heat and let cool for 10 minutes.

Preheat the oven to 350°F/180°C. Using your hands, squeeze out as much moisture from the thawed spinach as possible. Transfer the spinach into a large bowl, add the shallots, cheese, egg, herbs, and seasoning. Mix together well.

Halve each chicken breast and pound lightly to flatten each piece. Spoon some cheese mixture into the center of each piece, then roll them up. Wrap each roll in a slice of prosciutto and secure with a toothpick. Transfer to an ovenproof dish and dot with the remaining butter. Bake in the preheated oven for 30 minutes until golden.

Divide the baby spinach leaves among 4 serving plates. Remove the chicken from the oven and place 2 chicken rolls on each bed of spinach. Garnish with fresh chives and serve.

# Chicken Pinwheels with Bleu Cheese & Herbs

*serves 4*

2 tbsp pine nuts, lightly toasted

2 tbsp chopped fresh parsley

2 tbsp chopped fresh thyme

1 garlic clove, chopped

1 tbsp grated lemon zest

4 skinless, boneless chicken breasts

9 oz/250 g bleu cheese, crumbled

salt and pepper

mixed salad leaves, to serve

lemon slices and sprigs of fresh flat-leaf parsley, to garnish

Put the pine nuts into a food processor with the parsley, thyme, garlic, and lemon zest. Season with salt and pepper.

Pound the chicken breasts lightly to flatten them. Spread them on one side with the pine nut mixture, then top with the cheese. Roll them up from one short end to the other, so that the filling is enclosed. Wrap the rolls individually in aluminum foil, and seal well. Transfer into a steamer, or a metal colander placed over a pan of boiling water, cover tightly, and steam for 10–12 minutes, or until cooked through.

Arrange the salad leaves on a large serving platter. Remove the chicken from the heat, discard the foil, and cut the chicken rolls into slices. Arrange the slices over the lettuce leaves, garnish with slices of lemon and sprigs of parsley, and serve.

# Chicken & Veal Roll

*serves 4*

4 oz/115 g ground veal

4 skinless, boneless chicken breast portions, about 4½ oz/125 g each

1 cup Boursin or other cream cheese flavored with garlic and herbs

3 tbsp honey

salt and pepper

fresh sage leaves, to garnish (optional)

Put the ground veal in a pan and cook over medium–low heat, stirring frequently, for 5 minutes until evenly browned and broken up. Season with salt and pepper and remove the skillet from the heat. Let cool.

Preheat the oven to 375°F/190°C. Spread out a sheet of plastic wrap and place the chicken portions on top, side by side. Cover with another sheet of plastic wrap and beat gently with a meat mallet until the portions form a continuous sheet about ½ inch/1 cm thick.

Remove the chicken from the plastic wrap and spread the cheese over one side of it. Spoon the ground veal evenly over the top. Roll up the chicken from one short side and brush with the honey.

Place the chicken roll in a roasting pan and cook for 1 hour, or until tender and cooked through. Transfer the chicken roll to a cutting board and cut into thin slices.

Serve immediately garnished with sage leaves, if using.

# Chicken in Marsala Sauce

*serves 4*

2 tbsp all-purpose flour

4 skinless, boneless chicken breasts, sliced lengthwise

3 tbsp olive oil

²/₃ cup Marsala

2 bay leaves

1 tbsp butter

salt and pepper

freshly cooked rice, to serve

Mix the flour, salt, and pepper together on a large plate or in a plastic food bag. Add the chicken and toss to coat.

Heat the oil in a skillet over medium heat. Add the chicken and cook for about 4 minutes on both sides until tender. Remove from the skillet and keep warm.

Skim most of the fat from the skillet and pour in the Marsala. Add the bay leaves and boil for 1 minute, stirring well, then add the butter with any juices from the chicken and cook until thickened.

Return the chicken to the skillet and heat through. Serve immediately with freshly cooked rice.

# Pan-Fried Chicken with Golden Sauce

*serves 4*

2 mangoes

14 oz/400 g canned apricots in juice

4 tbsp unsalted butter

4 skinless, boneless chicken breasts, about 6 oz/175 g each

salt and pepper

cooked new potatoes sprinkled with snipped chives, to serve

Using a sharp knife, slice off the sides of the mangoes as close to the pits as possible. Cut through the flesh in the half shells in a criss-cross pattern, turn inside out, and cut off the flesh. Cut off any remaining flesh from the pits. Place in a food processor.

Drain the apricots, setting aside about 1 cup of the can juice. Put the apricots and reserved juice into the food processor and process until smooth. Pour the sauce into a small pan.

Melt the butter in a large, heavy-bottom skillet. Add the chicken and cook over medium–low heat, turning occasionally, for 15 minutes until golden all over and cooked through. Test by piercing the thickest part with the point of a sharp knife. If the juices run clear, the chicken is cooked.

Meanwhile, place the pan of sauce over low heat to warm through, but do not boil.

Slice the chicken portions diagonally and arrange on warmed serving plates. Spoon the sauce over them, season with salt and pepper, and serve immediately with new potatoes sprinkled with chives.

# Roasted Chicken with Sun-Blush Tomato Pesto

*serves 4*

4 skinless, boneless chicken breasts, about 1 lb 12 oz/800 g in total

1 tbsp olive oil

green salad, to serve

*for the red pesto*

4½ oz/125 g sun-blush tomatoes in oil (drained weight), chopped

2 garlic cloves, crushed

4 tbsp pine nuts, lightly toasted, plus extra for sprinkling

⅔ cup extra virgin olive oil

Preheat the oven to 400°F/200°C. To make the red pesto, put the sun-blush tomatoes, garlic, pine nuts, and oil into a food processor and process to a coarse paste.

Arrange the chicken in a large, ovenproof dish or roasting pan. Brush each breast with the oil, then place a tablespoon of red pesto over each breast. Using the back of a spoon, spread the pesto so that it covers the top of each breast. This pesto recipe makes more than just the 4 tablespoons used here. Store the extra pesto in an airtight container in the refrigerator for up to 1 week.

Roast the chicken in the preheated oven for 30 minutes, or until tender and the juices run clear when a skewer is inserted into the thickest part of the meat.

Sprinkle with the remaining pine nuts and serve with a green salad.

# Tarragon Chicken

*serves 4*

4 skinless, boneless chicken breasts, about 6 oz/175 g each

½ cup dry white wine

1–1¼ cups chicken stock

1 garlic clove, finely chopped

1 tbsp dried tarragon

¾ cup heavy cream

1 tbsp chopped fresh tarragon

salt and pepper

fresh tarragon sprigs, to garnish

sugar snap peas, to serve

Season the chicken with salt and pepper and place in a single layer in a large, heavy-bottom skillet. Pour in the wine and enough chicken stock just to cover and add the garlic and dried tarragon. Bring to a boil, reduce the heat, and poach gently for 10 minutes, or until the chicken is cooked through and tender.

Remove the chicken with a slotted spoon or tongs, cover, and keep warm. Strain the poaching liquid into a clean skillet and skim off any fat from the surface. Bring to a boil and cook until reduced by about two-thirds.

Stir in the cream, return to a boil, and cook until reduced by about half. Stir in the fresh tarragon. Slice the chicken breasts and arrange on warmed plates. Spoon over the sauce, garnish with tarragon sprigs, and serve immediately with sugar snap peas.

# Chili Chicken with Chickpea Mash

*serves 4*

4 skinless chicken breasts, about 5 oz/140 g each

1 tbsp olive oil

8 tsp harissa (chili) paste

salt and pepper

*for the chickpea mash*

2 tbsp olive oil

2–3 garlic cloves, crushed

14 oz/400 g no salt or sugar canned chickpeas, drained and rinsed

4 tbsp lowfat milk

3 tbsp chopped fresh cilantro, plus extra to garnish

salt and pepper

Make shallow cuts in each chicken breast. Place the chicken in a dish, brush with the olive oil, and coat both sides of each breast with the harissa paste. Season well with salt and pepper, cover the dish with foil, and let marinate in the refrigerator for 30 minutes.

Preheat the oven to 425°F/220°C. Transfer the chicken breasts to a roasting pan and roast for about 20–30 minutes until they are cooked through and there is no trace of pink in the center.

Meanwhile make the chickpea mash. Heat the oil in a pan and gently fry the garlic for 1 minute, then add the chickpeas and milk and heat through for a few minutes. Transfer to a blender or food processor and purée until smooth. Season to taste with salt and pepper and stir in the fresh cilantro.

To serve, divide the chickpea mash among 4 serving plates, top each one with a chicken breast, and garnish with cilantro.